BMP
8120

ASHES and ALL

poems by

Marjorie Deiter Keyishian

To Dear Barbara,
With Love,
Marge

DOS MADRES

2015

DOS MADRES PRESS INC.
P.O.Box 294, Loveland, Ohio 45140
www.dosmadres.com   editor@dosmadres.com

Dos Madres is dedicated to the belief that the small press is essential to the vitality of contemporary literature as a carrier of the new voice, as well as the older, sometimes forgotten voices of the past. And in an ever more virtual world, to the creation of fine books pleasing to the eye and hand.

Dos Madres is named in honor of Vera Murphy and Libbie Hughes, the "Dos Madres" whose contributions have made this press possible.

Dos Madres Press, Inc. is an Ohio Not For Profit Corporation and a 501 (c) (3) qualified public charity. Contributions are tax deductible.

Executive Editor: Robert J. Murphy

Illustration & Book Design: Elizabeth H. Murphy
www.illusionstudios.net

Typset in Adobe Garamond Pro & Deportees
ISBN 978-1-939929-37-2
Library of Congress Control Number: 2015941841

First Edition

ACKNOWLEDGEMENTS

"December 31," "Shiny Day," "Talking Birds," *Talisman* 43 (2015)

"Neighborhood," *Paterson Literary Review* 32 (2003)

"Deer Isle Cemetery," *Tiferet* (Feb-March 2007)

"Long Island Boneyard," *South Mountain Poets* (2006)

"Pacific Highway, Off 101" [as "As if his father"] *Footwork* (1989)

"David is Hiding," *Outerbridge* 3 (Fall 1978/Spring 1979)

To my two mothers, Rose and Arax

TABLE OF CONTENTS:

Among the Living

The Departed

Making Do

Among the Living

Birth

The way small particles
had to come together
and with huge contractions
explode into stars:
the tiny luck of egg, sperm,
toting all efflorescence
of past particles,
a sack of ancients,
women, men, dried up,
all that, there, in their uncurling.

But first,
the tiniest of swimming tadpoles
over, again, the first story.

II

And we didn't even know.
We, waiting here,
thinking we were whole,
could perceive a growing
but had no sense of their sweetness,
or the necessary trill of notes;
till the piping organ declare
the song, we did not know
how our aching ear would enchant us.

Ever after, the heart rounds outward
which thought its shape made,
the beat of it enough.

III

Plato's notion, the Idea whose
shadow is all we know of now: that's partial.
But always I was waiting
for the perfect,
the light of this child
curled, sleeping in the hollow
of my heart, waiting, waiting:
the thrust, push, final shove,
all that glistening, laborious oil
of becoming. So much labor
and it's forgotten in the wonder,
the lilt, the perfume of first blossoms,
the first harmonious joint,
sweet air, soft breeze, stir of new green
just uncurling. And one day every
branch is fringed in white, in pink,
the blossom; and, like blossoming,

I am anew who thought
my shape fixed forever.

Shiny Day

And then I dreamed it was the shiny day
of your wedding. A simple white dress, maybe
daisies, or do I invent them? You and I
walking through luminous green fields, singing
under the curving green leaves of dogwoods
hung with those delicate white flowers, perhaps a river
rippling blue against some flat white rock.

Two perhaps three hours, we strolled till, late, we
turned, quick as hares, back to catch wedding guests
fed, we hoped, so they would wait to see you
walking the petal-strewn path to marry.

So sweet a time, it kept the morn at bay.

Marbles

for Emily

Drop the cool rounds, the immies. Let them chime
but not chip as they dribble through calloused
fingers. Hold them one by one to the light,
the blue swirls in white, like precarious clouds,
too sweet to trade, they, glowing, are the spoils.

In the heat of the game, choose which one
to shoot next. You might lose, shoot too far or near.
Kneeling beside the map you drew in hard dirt,
you aim and aim again, weighing aggies.
Your fingers know the invisible flaws,
where bubbles push up against the tight arc.
Your muscles adjust the push. Taking time,
music of churning blood the drum that drowns
whistles, jeers, the wind itself, you shoot
and win, shoot and win. Every shot
easier, fingers learning the curve of the cup,
the sway of thin strips of packed earth
between sidewalk and gutter changed by rain,
changed by metal rims of pails, piled
with rotting detritus, emptied, and tossed back.

Store it safe, away, ever after,
in the dark corner, deep, under all
forgotten love letters, rubber-banded
batches in all shades of ink.

Which is the way? Quit or wager them:
the yellow and the blue, those, too,
immies, mibs, the yellow purie?

Playground

If you take a child to the playground,
he'll pause at the edge of blue space he says
is an ocean sea wherein odd creatures frolic.

He fills that sea with sea anemone.
They flower. You'll twirl, spin, tilt. You'll climb
a ladder to walk what might be treetop
height and slide down to spin again
as you catch the edge of what might
be a moon base, wherein are sheltered
sisters too small to climb themselves, boosted
to shelter, mid-disk, from the tilt and spin.

Drop off, and you're back in the flat world
where the phone rings. Friends drop off,
they sicken and die.

And you are left tunneling back,
to when you and they would run, shout, hide
from he who hid his eyes, and then
you could run back. All you had to do
was to touch base and shout Home Free All.
"Ollie Ollie Oxen Free"

Once Upon a Time

Once upon a time I hung out the wash,
borrowing three lines, filling four with the bonnets,
ruffled dresses, socks, lacy diaper covers
I'd dressed you in three or four times a day.
They smelled of the sea wind we two walked through,
you bouncing in your stroller, past the TB
hospital, pale shades looking out as we passed.
We never waved, so round and complete we were,
except for the sea that bubbled up almost to us
and away again and away, up and away.

Turn in the Road

In bird song, she took the turn in the road
far beyond where the eye could follow,
where it ran besides meadows,
meander of streams. She saw the swan's
neck curve, even as the road bent,
so that its black eye could find reflected
a white bird, gliding across glass.
And on the round island they would
find the selves, licked by falling blossoms
of fruiting cherries, plums, spring.

Where I Grew Up Were Sparrows

Where I grew up were sparrows, gulls,
your all-year-round birds. Come spring,
red breasted robins reappeared, first
the guys, then all of them, hanging out.

Salt on a tail to catch the bird. But how?
In blue shells babes break open,
beaks asking for worms or seed. I
don't know which will sate them,
the hungry young, the ravenous
young.

Here, goldfinches, red finches,
mob our feeders, chickadees fly,
arrows from the crested titmice
and the clowns, nuthatches
hanging upside-down peeking
in at us as deer do, a foot from
our kitchen window, wide
brown deer eyes perceiving what?

Neighborhood

Side by side, we grew
in high-stooped, narrow
houses, mirrors running down one
side and up the other, so that we
hung face to face, staring past the self
into another. While behind the houses were
scarves of perfect green, divided by hedge
after clipped hedge,
a city block of backyards abstractedly receding,
with enough leaves and trees and grasses to feed
cacophonies of squabbling sparrows
and a pair of robins, March after March.

Last Dance

So golden and dying, leaves trees release
hang, dry edges hooked to some spinning stream
of air. Waiting a summer for this dream
of flight, hex of fall, for green's end, they seize
what wind there is and ride. Red others wait
the final shiver of separation,
the radiant dance of disintegration.

Soaring through this reign of leaves, brown geese, late
of the north, pause, parade, natter and honk.
Red as leaves, cheeky children roil the leaves,
race the geese. Nothing so lovely can be
dying. Always overhead, golden oaks
will arch, leaves caught and falling, ring necked geese
and children ever under a lilting tree.

Scattered

Spread across the country, we might as well
be yellow leaves, letting go of an old oak
or reds from sugar maples. Here, skeleton branches
hinge naked to the sky. Chickadees settle there.

But we are so far apart, I cannot find
what it was like to spread lace across table
and table and we all seated round cauldrons
of soup, the great brown bird, the sweets,
pumpkins, chestnuts, yellow corn bread.
Most delicious was the all of us.

How I miss
you and you and you and the littles who
dance here and there and now so far away.

Sailing the Hudson

Gulls must, I think, have hooted
as they swooped low over the wake,
laughing at peels, heels of bread,
tuna encased in mayonnaise.
But the noises I remember
are the creak of rope and sail
flap of stiffening canvas.
Beside us warehouses flaunt
rococo shutters.
Harbor derelicts, flaking paint,
piers lean into the Hudson,
crowding the waves so that they hop aboard.

This ship is old but steady
a squat grandma, corsets creaking, rolling up
over the pavement on laced shoes,
ignoring time and the islands,
ignoring the jeering seagulls.
When she shifts course,
heeling into the wind,
we could slip between the rails
or fall right over the top, hit the grey river
where it merges with sea
to sail down, down, deep where
no one ever counts the days or years.

She ferries us out the mouth,
and then we turn skirting
sentinel islands, ignoring tides,
to where the great liners
once rode over waves that lift us
out of time, and drop us back,
into the ordinary shops, stalls,
snarls of afternoon, the sun setting,
the dark coming down.

And candles
you lit for me, guttering
in a wind that will scatter us
as naturally the red and yellow
leaves of the season drop and blow
this way and that, crumbling where
they fall, that, gallant as pennants,
fluttered in honor of our embarking.

Firefly

A stone lion, a wooden dog and there,
a flickering firefly, just one. Wait, a yard
away another—or does the one alone repeat
its signal light to no effect? Fireflies should be
everywhere, blinking all round and high above
so that we here can't tell the one bright star
from another yearning firefly.

Budding trees form an aisle filled I fear with nests
of lyme ticks. Sun dappled streams hide leeches,
blood suckers that cling as legs emerge.
Afflicted by fungus, our bats who dine
on whining mosquitoes, die off, noses
wrapped in wet grey killing fuzz.
Even as dogwood bloom white tinged
with pink draping glorious boughs wide overhead
and underfoot, soft moss pillows every step.

Talking Birds

At dawn, bird after bird calls out. I hear
that chat, those assertions, that hold
onto, that claim one oak or another,
that call, friend to friend, or lover,
whichever. I am a part of the talk
that starts just before five and cheers me,
so I can wake or fall back deep into sleep
filled with dream after dream that can enchant
or weave what is with what I need to know.
Or else entwine this worry, this knot, tale
that tackles all, entangles. But bird talk
rescues me, morn after morn, if just for now.

Could a Night Go By?

Could a night go by without a single
dream? Flat grey from deep black to the feisty five
a.m singing, calling, squabbling birds. They
insist there is something worth argument,
a daily bustle to fortify nest,
to defend it, to feed insistent beaks open
in first light and oh, so, hungry. Nestlings
who want a life, no matter how spare,
who will fly away so far, as if no
nest had ever nurtured them, to build
anew, some sunny morning when spring
comes early, blossoming even as the sun
blares its bright assertion that this, some
other, day will flare, spiky orange,
yellow. Anything but ordinary.

Telling Tales

Landing on desert shore, a rocky place
where hermit crab mimics spider: all
of it pure magic, this coming back. Awake,
it's morning; still I'm searching, searching,
when I know quite well: the dead are dead,
white as lamb bone or turkey leg, picked clean
as the skeleton fish lifted from poached trout,
translucent as the spine structure I hold
up where it catches light. Were a canvas
there, it would catch a shadow remnant.

The helter-skelter of my white frame,
fitted together once upon this time,
makes no sense by dawn. Earthen, a brown rectangle,
a hollow rectangle filled still with spectral black,
should have been made of the coffin wood,
but is magically of crumbling earth from which,
maybe, a clay-molding maker produced you and me.

True, those bones should have yellowed as teeth do,
turned brown as the tea we drank
and drank. No fleck of flesh was left,
only the dirt and the meaningless
scatter spat of lonely remnant bone.

Harvest

Raccoons ingeniously finger a way
between lid and can and then
they knock over pails, drag them across
the porch in a perfectly reasonable quest
for carrot peelings, corn cobs, chicken bones,
a harvest that you and I would not
deny them, were they to clean up after themselves.

Epicureans in our garden,
they bite once into every cuke,
once into every tomato, and pass on.

My rage is out of keeping, you say.
But remember the delicate spray of leaves
I, bent, bitten, and parched, have been tending
all through the hot August, wherein one
day was worse than the last and nothing
but dying fall to look forward to.

Spider Woman

Arachnids, spinning intricacy,
sparkling frames on which rain drops,
inspire this huge metal apostrophe
I pose beside
precisely modeled on the tiny spinner
at my kitchen window whose eggs
hold more and more of the brown spiders
whose bites might be fatal.
Nonetheless, I search them out, the huge metal
replicas, the cement incarnations. I stand
beside you, modeling, now as you do.

Talking Wood

On the first blue day, birds write north
all over the sky, except for these robins.
One or two to a branch, they layer blue
spruce and pine whose limbs form skeletal
arabesques, delicate backbones,
sending loop after wooden loop
high and higher. In those wooden arches,
I can read the vertebrae of curly
cabbage leaves, and perhaps those great discs
of wheeling stars also echo
the delicate joining of rib to spine,
the web of twig breathing green
out of the chubby buds, packed
tightly with leaf and leaf
reveling in the rite to uncurl.

No one need remember the rain,
freezing as it fell,
or the wind that came up one day
when every twig was weighed down, crystal
branches catching moonlight, so that
they chimed, glowing yellow, then pink
with the dawn, before they broke.

Written in these woods, for anyone to read,
are that hordes of seedlings struggled,
trees bent, as they tunneled up
at whatever angle—to where the sun
shines, a point in the dark, and above
they open; that rustling green song
filling heartwood, and roots and all.

Written in the fallen spruce
shielding the rooting seed,
written in the oak that has no need
to remember the ring upon ring of lean
years and kind soaking rain and sun
just above the hundred thousand curlicues.
that the velvet green of August night
dissolves to feed grub, earth,
and nesting bird is written in thick
layers underfoot, of leaf and thin blue shell.

The Departed

Ashes and All

The ashes of how many fires were white
in the hearth, pillows of ash, bundles of ash.
Call them ghosts of dust who flared a fierce red,
threatening to leap out of the hearth as once
they battered at the roof, asking us what we did
so small, so fragile, when they stood forty foot
rooted deep, ring upon ring of hard wood.

I could have scattered the ash to feed earth,
but it was cold and I unwilling to put on glove,
scarf, jacket. Now from the muddy earth, I pluck
twig and branch the wind and rain have dropped. A cage
of kindling, over and again, and log upon log.

My friends quaver as they walk. They teeter
white as those ashes I shoveled from the hearth.
And over in Haiti, the hurt lie under the usual
indifferent sky. The shattered port littered with
the fallen, entombing they say 50,000 of what
were vital just a week ago. The smell of the rotting
dead afflicts survivors hurrying out of the city.

My daughters deliver frail infants whose
tangled blood turns them yellow or born
too early they lie taped to machines
that read what signs there are, heartbeats.

Icicles

Within the icicles that hang down
are whole globes, three disparate worlds,
one beneath the other, and more.
The shag of them, of icicles
dripping down, they coalesce,
even as you disappeared,
even as, remembering the stone other,
the stalactite, you and I enter
again the classroom where we learned
that what hung down in caves had one
name and what grew up, another.
Stalagmites, pink and white, I found
so far far away, deep under Blue Mountain,
across the wide, wide Pacific.

Here, a shapely translucence
catches light, even as melting, changing,
to once again, the running water
birds want. And stone is no more sure
than you, who walked pavement and beach
and now are nowhere.

Dreamscape

You surface. We are mates again.
As old as I, you wear the face I knew
full fifty years ago. You've come back
from somewhere, Europe perhaps, weeping,
your belly big with a first child
I wonder at. The flat we shared sparkles.
At long last, here, deep in black night
I will discover what became of you
who knew so well, who knew so much,
oh, so much better than I, how to move
through, manipulate, this wide world.

Awake, all day long, I climb those old stairs.
Bookbag over my shoulder, I can even
look out at a rare lighted window. Why,
my dear, perhaps you haunt this October
night, too. One of us might be a conjurer,
plucking up those lustful days so today
stretches to contain both ancient cracked
pavements and the leafy yard I rake.

Central Park

Any tree choked with feeding leaves
can be pulled from brown earth.
Shrouded in that black cloud come
down from the north bearing heavy rain
that beats against those leaves, that sucks
roots loose, drowns them so they let fall
the great oak, or just one branch drops,
and underneath buries the child hiding there.
The death of the limb, the tree, and what
stands beneath, sheltering there, head resting
against the shaggy bark, that dark center
that held, should hold, all green in place.

Deer Isle Cemetery

Should we all elect to return
after the last sweet breath
to this tumble of thin, grey stones,
listing in sea wind, odd lives and short,
etched or scratched, the shallow letters
telling the times but fading, blending
with lichen and chips, we would need
to negotiate, make an offer, buy the land.

New graves would stretch under the fencing trees,
so many that we would challenge grove after
grove, and the earth would roll, I think,
where the coffins rot, and sink,
where silently the rain,
where the frost, where the heave
of winter take hold. And untroubled,
the birds would sing lusty orisons,
the seagulls scream. Leaves would cover
us over, and in a little while,
no one, nearby, would know
when we came or from where.

In summer, survivors might picnic.
Resting their heads against the grass, they'd
turn to read the stories, the lives, the times,
and learn to dig deep into granite—
if they expect the ever after.

Long Island Bone Yard

That necropolis, crowded as Manhattan,
and as lively, awaits, names inscribed on gates,
whole neighborhoods laid out, the lanes
named for trees: Wisteria, Lilac, Oak.
To get there, we travel in cavalcades—
(short if we live long, long if we die young)
pausing to pay tolls. Headlights identify
those who grieve from the many in a hurry,
ordinary folk, zipping in and out,
superstitious but late, companions as
they weave in and out, behind the hearse
proceeding at a lively pace to the gate,
that marks our plot, acquired long ago,
already full of uncles, aunts, cousins,
and in some distant corner Sarah & Max,
and all their congregation.

Shoulder to shoulder, dancing or dueling,
here, entrenched, stretching, forever—
stretching as far as the eye can see,
tended daily by men who
have nothing to do with us, except to dig
the corner marked on their map, D6,
just where Acacia meets Maple.
The silent processions roll out, two, three,
at a time, along the neck of the ugly isle,
Neighbors pile healing stone upon stone—
sometimes, even dropping the spare pebble
on strangers' graves.

Our plot, furnished with a stone bench,
mellow with lichen, half-hidden by mulberry,
name engraved solemnly in marble,
and one narrow space, filled. And stretching
for acres, for miles, stones and stones
planted where once potatoes grew,
the flat field regenerating under our feet.

December Thirty-One

The year is falling apart. Each year does
will us to die with it. We must invoke
the gold we know: moonlight as lucid
as silver foil, wax candles as gold,
as red, as the sun once was, long days ago.

If we wake early, it is to darkness.
The real children must be told it's morning.
Light comes later, and then it's thin, watery,
unconvincing—a brief interval
in a continuum which is the night,
naturally black; the holes that are stars
too far gone to be more than a story
we invented some time ago, winter's
infant, in which we must believe, the light.

Chaos Theory

An irregular fringe of icicles,
the long and short of chaos hanging, edging
the eaves, that coalescence, that deterioration,
as predictable as two plus two,
no more mysterious than ketchup,
engages the eye and with dense tangle of twigs
encased in white ice that fill grey sky
simply delights, even as we huddle inside.
Sparrows flit. Titmouse and chickadee feed.
Icicles melt. Elsewhere streets fill with mobs
that pelt each other with rocks, under a hot sun.
By night, streets will empty: curfew. The cold,
perhaps, will trim eaves over again. Thin
crystals might, for a time, sparkle in chill sunlight.

Carolina Parakeet – Now Extinct

About the dead, my dead, they multiply,
don't they, as we age. Even as evenings
fill with honeysuckle, pink, chickadee song,
siren shriek of a red-winged blackbird
spiraling into crystal black, star-speckled
before the moon rises, all round,
and blossoms vibrate white in moonshine.

Had you but flit past a window
or perched on a branch of the improbable
peach tree, planted with pits we pitched,
growing askew beside a cinder-block wall,
then, oh, then, you would become manifest
now, as all my other dead do, sweet faces
flickering on when I come again to a place,
where they or he or she laughed or lounged
or lifted crystal goblet filled with wine-dark sea.

Byways

Passing through, you ask: what do they do here,
in this empty place, whose lawns touch this road,
and nothing (but the season) changes?
We are learning the language of animals:
the panic of the fat, nibbling rabbits,
the last long shrieks of the rabid fox.
Fireflies are spelling the name of their kind.
Our tongues will know secret, silky places
that honeysuckles spit out at dusk.
By day, we jack up our wooden houses
to mend stone foundations; we scrape blisters
of paint away; we use yellow anew.
Walls of our rooms are hung with words we mine.
Nightly, we listen as the lights go out.

The Amaryllis

The amaryllis has opened yellow-tipped
petals red as the cardinal who eats
oily seeds a green planter spills for him.
A hill glistens; pillow after pillow of snow lit
at the rim sparkles. The deer trek past the plum tree
to drink at the stony grey bird bath.
And when knife edge of sun sets, turns all soft
then blue-lit, then the dark will swallow all.

Shifting a Hill

Were you here, you would have seen
the yellow Deere scooping up a hill,
taking it quite away, making flatness happen.
Shovel by delicate shovel fills, the pointed
edges picking up grain by rich brown grain
making a high mound of fragrant earth that took
an eon to cover the shelf of stone on which
we built our shingled houses, aslant, street
warping what we thought was solid ground.
The graceful swinging yellow claw shifts
what was to what will be, for some little while.

You who have taken apart your house
to put it back together strong and solid
do not need to watch the earth slide away.
You can imagine carving the earth, as if
it were some turkey, into serving-sized portions.

I who look back at the yellow house
eaten by flame and all the meals we
ate there become the dust that
happens when beloved people die
must marvel at the way high hills go away.

David is Hiding

The Arno's shrunk. What's left is thin and brown,
a rag of a river. Weeds taller than man,
weeds rooted on white islands, grow under
these silly bridges.

The white brides of Florence
are hiding in shops or sleeping the steamy
sleep of hot afternoons. The city's for sale,
squares draped in scarves, tooled leather bags,
sun glasses. Swarthy young men and huge bees
are busy, loud, and everywhere. Shadows
hot and the sun ferocious, Medicis
crumbling behind closed doors hidden by tall
piles of straw hats. To walk these broad streets,
to cross that fiery piazza, finding a way
through wagons of merchandise, is exhausting.

Somewhere David in his high cool hall is hiding.
One iron grey winter's day, the rain
and the river will plot a new course,
will find the door, will eat his strong hands,
his fine sinewy thighs and sliding back
to its banks will take him along.

No one will notice, I think.
Perhaps that old man, taking the small steps
his crippled joints let him, helped and mocked
by the market men, has mind enough left
to remember the dangerous giant,
the arms and the eye that defeated him,
the rock, and David's long, cool limbs.

Salvage

If, some centuries ago, midway in Russia
wherein our peoples were, for once, cheek to jowl,
I chose you, you me: an enchantment, a spell…
is to forget infants thrown alive. Ma and pa,
whole families consumed in ovens, those sold
into bondage, a holocaust of ashes, of lonely lost.

Ah, but shadows slant across the dappled grass.
Somewhere a small brown bird sings, and we
who have the shining, winding morning glory
must salute this fragile moment as if it were
all and forever, lighting if we can, single
candles that recall the one, the each, the all,
lest they and we lose even this.

Indifference

A dimpling tide, frolicking at my toes,
can climb forty stories, sweep ashore, level
all we built, all we planted, wash away
a passing train, taking with it, back to sea,
tiny newborn and her aged grandma
gone out to sea or left, poor battered shells,
to swell or rot under the blind sun. Tide
must go as uneven heaving molten core
insists. Nor can you ask wind to hold off.
It blows circles, lifts dirt, strips bark, knocks
apart what you thought were brick havens
as easily as wolf blew down straw house,
if without wolf's hunger. Wind and water
have that indifference in common.

But you and I, my child, have modulation:
the power to think before we shriek,
to hold back before we blow apart,
to make bright as a giggle this dark day.

September

A riot of green, exuberance,
call it frenzy. Branches loop, they sway.
Green leaves slide like satin across
the skin. I could bathe in the green space
of it, if I climb just high enough to become
one with the green of them, the riot of leaves
that has grown up to occupy even the sky.

Departures

I think first the ship sails with you and you.
Then you are in the corners of the town
where you marketed. What becomes of us?
Dissolution. And after that, do we twinkle,
elbows of scattered atoms out there from where
I promised I would send down my love
when they, my beloveds, need it?

I hate most early departures, you and you.
Some made good escapes just as the body
withered and the mind went elsewhere.

The mourning dove is in fact looking for
a mate, the one other that will, together,
create what never has been. It never will be.
That sad call is merely seduction, the new
spring is the first and only, the singular one
as you were or are the essence I will always miss.

Daytime Parrots

Here squawking, daytime parrots replace
the night-time, big-eared, ring-tailed possums
and the north wind whines, whistles, harries
leaves rising, blowing, branches a-dancing.
North is hot, full of spores. Thunder blasts
out of that desert north. Note that under us
the earth might sink. Step carefully,
lest we fall through, right through, a pillowing round
of blue Pacific to where we were,
you are, snow-white and real.

Remember

As if the whole were laid out, a round of times,
and I a skater whooshing back and forward
on that flat, frozen lake. Now and then someone
emerges full grown and ever after is there,
a zig-zag of fur.

The sea tumbled Penny out just a week ago.
She rides what waves, curls, peeps, threatened
by strep, by meningitis—sharks swimming here
despite sanitized nurses all in white. Too weak
to eat. From the shattered shards to take with me.

Dolphin's Return

Dolphin, walking on water, dancing,
as Christ could not, unreproving,
at the edge, took the step, plunged.

Did you hesitate, let waves bubble
between unwebbed feet, troubled,
tempted--all crowded on a sliver
of moony shore wondering, aquiver
with time gone under hot sun, heavy air?

Did one pause at the edge of a cliff
mourning and all caught--his transcendence
a radiating impulse travelling in widening
circles--the species turning, one by one,
each leaving a pot, a plant behind,
each embarking, plunging, buoyed
by love under the buoyant water?

Your abandoned cities, doors
and windows of strange fishy shapes,
are crumbling, hieroglyphics, codes,
unbroken. Who is left to read them?
Long ago, Odysseus at Ithaca flickered
out; telegraphers retired.

Out wandering,
I have heard high piping,
the laugh of, the call of dolphins.

Pacific Highway, Off 101

Icarus, flying the pure blue space,
did not know he was doomed to splat
red against the blue sea,
meat for sardines, sea worms, and crabs.
He dove, instead, into earth, 4 square,
mistaking for the blue Pacific,
the syncopated whoosh of cars
that clog the grey macadam border,
called the Pacific Highway, off 101.

He left his red-eyed dad behind, his eyes blurred,
his voice high and wound tight,
the worst having happened already.
Dad does not know why to put the one foot
in front, then the other. His shaky hand
has to hold up the mother, as well,
made so heavy by loss,
that she sinks deeper into the earth
with every step.

Dad who always turns back to make sure
the old dog doesn't wander away, saw
him roped to machines. They do absolutely
everything, worse than the grave.
Who will look after dad now that you've
ridden away, visor down,
motorcycle warrior, helmeted,
in your leather gauntlets?
A briefcase, strapped to your back,
was stuffed with pappety pap,
so you outraced it. It tore open
and, flutter, flutter, all gone.
Was it the deadly ordeal of soap,

stacked as if
which one made a difference,
the littered streets, vapid windows,
the melancholy vistas of lawns
baked flat as matzos?

My sweet Marc, eyes bluer than cornflowers
waddle-walker who forgot somewhere
how to crow without cussing,
that you rot under a thin wormy sheet
a gardener straightens and greens
nothing can heal.

What is Better?

What is better than a clean white page?
The snow curling around rock edges
piling soft billows where we walk
near knee deep. Great black birds that
drop down to feast upon whatever perished,
there, at the edge of Little Goose island.
Nothing goes to waste. We carrion eaters
clean away the flesh, polish the bones.
Our small ones slide down the hills we groom
for them. Their bright red sleds, as sharp as teeth,
smooth the earth we feed seed by seed in spring.
And in time we dig far down, hollow out
a final table for the many hungry worms.

Scribbling Shadows

Shadows write leaves on fat tree trunks.
Behind us, they follow
aslant atop distorting rocks and then--
stretching this way and that, thin black
echo of you and me—
climb steepest hills,
slide right over the rippling sea.

Peddles churn beside the bay:
push up, push down, slide along,
pass Sand Beach, where horseshoes
shuffle up from the sea
as far as tide line lets them.

First trill of sweet white,
whirr of spinning tire,
mourning doves whoo whoo,
speaking birds, owl hoot caws.
Crows chatter at one another.

Once upon a time, a bent, black-suited
man sang out, "I buy old clothes" all down
the street on a very hot day.

Midroad, the yellow cart pauses.
A tinkle of ice man,
chocolate, lemon, orange, lime.
Just after the belching garbage truck,
a clatter of emptying cans flung.

Bark, bark, brown bark,
tattoo of kids' feet hitting dirt, pavement,
the wooden slats of bridge, reverberating
as they run, skip, take giant steps.

The Iron Gate Left Open

We rode its black curlicues, swung,
side by side. Alas, our weight, you plus me, tugged
out rivets, bent hinges. That gate hangs
askew. And we, chagrinned, have turned good.

One bad day that yellow house caught fire, burned
bright as a Sabbath candle, Metal gate running
red, streaming through burning grass to sand.
All jumble, house become
ash just fiery minutes later.
Overhead the red light churning
around and around.

A lighthouse, ever after:
a beam of yellow house to bring
me safe through oh decades of storm
home to where, gate gone, house sunk
to ash somewhere under.

Over it is raised a squat brick gravestone,
a story high, wherein strangers spin, noisy
strangers tumble out of a brown door,
strangers occupy pavement, roller-skate,
shouting, down the street. Mamas,
arms crossed over full bosoms,
gossip, sing, each to each.

Under them, coal Max shoveled rattles
down the chute sparkling black lumps.
Warmed, we caught cups of that hot air
as it rose through metal grates.

Once, barred windows let in shadow.
Twilight, knee high legs walked by, shoes.
The barred window let in the "I cash old clothes"
chant of the cursing black sacked peddler,
the jingle of the yellow ices, pink,
chocolate. Fruit man, fish man.
Clop of a horse, wheeze, sneeze,

The barred window let in light that hit
lumps of shiny salmon-pink bedspread,
the gilded framed Grand Canyon,
lit tiny climbers, lit lost Indians.
In some shadowy corner, a cathedral
radio cries brown.

The gate swings. I'll follow, one day. We have
the gate and beyond, a yellow house
      reaching up and up to where
the star light is sun enough
      to stripe the sky.

The gate gapes open.

To Grandmother's House

We are noisy riding the swings
hung for us in the walled, city garden.
Time's between us, if death were not.

The young wife in a new yellow
house puts up preserves. Jars of purple
plums line shelves. They waver as memory
loses the shape of the pantry. The coil
of her red hair at her neck sheds pins.

The black-coated old line park benches,
nodding to us as we skip past. They
turn to monuments, close
as ever. The town they brought with them
is the map of this stone park we plant.

I wasn't looking the day I closed
the door. Corners I didn't turn
to study loom, dissolve, lose squareness.
Once a year, we drink the wine she made.

If I turn back, find the black gate,
the bench where my mother, framed
in silver, sits, I'll be behind
hedges and barred windows, asleep

or listening to these footsteps
clicking closer, this knock at the door,
loosed from a sleep I wasn't ready for.

Grandmother's at the door.
I don't know her. I never did.
Trolley tracks are at the corner;
the house has never been torn down.

Making Do

I Watch

Across the lake red maple flares
beside and above a golden oak.
But I must watch where I walk lest I fall.
When candles burn down, then flicker out,
there is light all the while, so this dimming
of my eyes is more like twilight. Moment
by moment, the sky turns. First it's white. The
graying comes after, quicker and quicker
as fall turns to winter and darkness
threatens to take more: one final turn.

Losing Sight of

I read a word letter by letter,
sometimes inventing, sometimes deciphering.
Nonetheless, what you meant is, day by day,
small and smaller. Now is the year's dark time
and if you go so far away, what then?
I still can see billowing snow sparkle,
and boles, brown, brown shaggy trunks. A rattle
of withered leaves, there, I hear. They hold on
to tell the new froth of green where to grow
and how. Is there a point when cold wind blows
shifting me as I lean into it? Look
how it combs my hair. What now holds me here?

My Eyes Don't See the Dead

Luckily, my eyes don't see the dead.
As if we weren't here, slantwise, the sea
sweeps in, circles, breaking as if we weren't here.
Not an island out there. Somewhere down our road,
hollowed out from this hill, rocks we named Apostles
have stood despite it. Now they crumble as rocks must.
Not that sea is implacable; simply ocean rolls on,
just on, salt blur, deep blue, then aqua
dimpling white, sea is coming, where Australia
happens to be, for a time.

Controlled Falling

Walking is controlled falling, they say,
who watch the crawler lift herself
skyward and cruise the length of the table,
letting go just so long as it takes
to step couchward. And one bright day
she lets go, steps out once, and then
again, wobbling as she holds onto air,
just air.
Ever after she walks, still
with the wobble, until it is just what
she does. And there's no wonder left in it. But I,
I now know, the risk is there in stepping
down. Even stepping out may mean a pitch,
a fall, the cracked hip, elbow, knee.
But, my friend, hold on, perhaps to my hand.

On a Rainy Sunday

On a rainy Sunday, I salute machines
that pick up squiggles, an alphabet gone
elsewhere, taking away the cotton candy
of words, nightingales, the spinning universe
quite gone, along with all those numbers
straining to tell me how many and when
to become.

What Stands Beneath

But if the bough breaks, what stands under
the shattering limb, sheltering there, head resting
against the shaggy bark, that dark center
that, till now, held, should hold, all green in place?
The tree and what stands beneath,
slipping down, sliding away, fainting,
that fall rehearses that final turning off.

Investigate the space, the tilt, the slide,
and the dark. Others may slide out of their
bodies, leaving emptiness, vacant space.
Did he, the man that sat in a chair, still sitting,
here in this pine-framed room flooded with light?

My emptying out will be the fading away of words.
The stories that held the wide world together
will not spin themselves out, catching hold
of the sleeve, winding up and around. You say
I will remember, but that shell tells me otherwise.

I am catching hold of what words I see,
hugging them close as they spill out, as they spell.

Thirty-one October

Those skeletons rattling at the front door
are not withered leaves fallen late. Remnants
make some other kind of noise. These rowdy
snickers are not of the candy crowd—ah, no.
Old friends time took away in his sack are
rattling bony fingers, calling for you
and me, as once, at back doors, they knuckled
the windows to wake us. Parents snoring a bed
away, and we with all the wide green morning
to the ocean over clammy sand. Why, later,
the crowds and the brand of the sun would eat
our day, melt cream sticks, poison crabs that last
night's tide forgot; and now, you and I are
remnants the old crowds come to call for, alas.

✦ Dance with my Shadow

I dance with my shadow: forget transience.
All down the hill leaves weave and I am black
shadow, wearing artful edges that dance.
We sway as one. I think I can rise with them,
become the green permanence hitched to bowing branches.
So full of sap and wind, we will never wither.
Somewhere a lilac exhales, and we are all
asway. Is it waltzing if it was, long
before that dance was named, our dance?
Are we naming rhythms, the reflections of how
the heart beats, the wind blows the sinuous leaves?

And the black cat rolls in the sun,
stretching so every muscle purrs

Meditation

That strutting woodpecker is drilling
there on succulent grubs,
who are nested in the wood
that sheathes this house
that keeps us dry, warm.

Lili's bones jut out. Her bright green
eyes shine above her pointed chin.
She calls and calls, imperiously orders:
pat me, feed me, pat me, for a bit,
a little while, a little, little while.

Tidal Flood Warning

Back then, the swollen
heart filled the chest so full
it threatened to break open.
We wanted, lusted, or loved.

Now, small strokes, brittle arteries
afflict a fading heart, that failing pump,
ah, and what of the brain
so stuffed with you and me
draining, yes, very like the spinning vortex,
disappearing. Is that day, and this
soon after, that face and mine,
who you will remember? What will I pick?

ABOUT THE AUTHOR

MARJORIE DEITER KEYISHIAN is the author of two poetry chapbooks: *Slow Runner* (Finishing Line Press, 2007) and *Demeter's Daughters* (Pudding House Publications, 2010). Her poems have appeared in a number of journals, including *The Massachusetts Review*, *Graham House Review*, *The Literary Review*, *The Laurel Review*, *South Mountain Poets*, *Black Mountain II Review*, *New York Quarterly*, *Tiferet*, *Paterson Literary Review*, *Snowy Egret*, *Northeast Journal*, *The Smith*, *Outerbridge* and *The Journal of New Jersey Poets*. For many decades, she taught literature and writing courses at Fairleigh Dickinson University in Madison, New Jersey. Born in Brooklyn, New York and married to Harry Keyishian, she has four daughters and seven grandchildren.

Books by Dos Madres Press

Mary Margaret Alvarado - *Hey Folly* (2013)

John Anson - *Jose-Maria de Heredia's Les Trophées* (2013),
    Time Pieces - poems & translations (2014)

Jennifer Arin - *Ways We Hold* (2012)

Michael Autrey - *From The Genre Of Silence* (2008)

Paul Bray - *Things Past and Things to Come* (2006), *Terrible Woods* (2008)

Ann Cefola - *Face Painting in the Dark* (2014)

Tom Cheetham - *Boundary Violations* (2015)

Jon Curley - *New Shadows* (2009), *Angles of Incidents* (2012)

Grace Curtis - *The Shape of a Box* (2014)

Sara Dailey - *Earlier Lives* (2012)

Dennis Daly - *Nightwalking with Nathaniel-poems of Salem* (2014)

Richard Darabaner - *Plaint* (2012)

Deborah Diemont - *Wanderer* (2009), *Diverting Angels* (2012)

Joseph Donahue - *The Copper Scroll* (2007)

Annie Finch - *Home Birth* (2004)

Norman Finkelstein - *An Assembly* (2004), *Scribe* (2009)

Karen George - *Swim Your Way Back* (2014)

Gerry Grubbs - *Still Life* (2005), *Girls in Bright Dresses Dancing* (2010),
    The Hive-a book we read for its honey (2013)

Richard Hague - *Burst, Poems Quickly* (2004),
    During The Recent Extinctions (2012)

Ruth D. Handel - *Tugboat Warrior* (2013)

Pauletta Hansel - *First Person* (2007), *What I Did There* (2011)

Michael Heller - *A Look at the Door with the Hinges Off* (2006),
    Earth and Cave (2006)

Michael Henson - *The Tao of Longing & The Body Geographic* (2010)

R. Nemo Hill - *When Men Bow Down* (2012)

W. Nick Hill - *And We'd Understand Crows Laughing* (2012)

Eric Hoffman - *Life At Braintree* (2008), *The American Eye* (2011),
    By The Hours (2013)

James Hogan - *Rue St. Jacques* (2005)

Keith Holyoak - *My Minotaur* (2010), *Foreigner* (2012)

Nancy Kassell - *Text(isles)* (2013)

David M. Katz - *Claims of Home* (2011)

Sherry Kearns - *Deep Kiss* (2013), *The Magnificence of Ruin* (2015)

Burt Kimmelman - *There Are Words* (2007), *The Way We Live* (2011)

Jill Kelly Koren - *The Work of the Body* (2015)

Ralph La Charity - *Farewellia a la Aralee* (2014)

Pamela L. Laskin - *Plagiarist* (2012)

Owen Lewis - *Sometimes Full of Daylight* (2013)

Richard Luftig - *Off The Map* (2006)

Austin MacRae - *The Organ Builder* (2012)

Mario Markus - *Chemical Poems-One For Each Element* (2013)

J. Morris - *The Musician, Approaching Sleep* (2006)

Patricia Monaghan - *Mary-A Life in Verse* (2014)

Rick Mullin - *Soutine* (2012), *Coelacanth* (2013),
    Sonnets on the Voyage of the Beagle (2014)

Fred Muratori - *A Civilization* (2014)

Robert Murphy - *Not For You Alone* (2004), *Life in the Ordovician* (2007),
    From Behind The Blind (2013)

Pam O'Brien - *The Answer To Each Is The Same* (2012)

Peter O'Leary - *A Mystical Theology of the Limbic Fissure* (2005)

Bea Opengart - *In The Land* (2011)

David A. Petreman - *Candlelight in Quintero-bilingual ed.* (2011)

Paul Pines - *Reflections in a Smoking Mirror* (2011),
    New Orleans Variations & Paris Ouroboros (2013),
    Fishing on the Pole Star (2014)
    Message from the Memoirist (2015

William Schickel - *What A Woman* (2007)

Don Schofield - *In Lands Imagination Favors* (2014)

David Schloss - *Behind the Eyes* (2005)

Daniel Shapiro - *The Red Handkerchief and other poems* (2014)

Murray Shugars - *Songs My Mother Never Taught Me* (2011),
    Snakebit Kudzu (2013)

Jason Shulman - *What does reward bring you but to bind you to Heaven like a slave? (2013)*

Maxine Silverman - *Palimpsest (2014)*

Lianne Spidel & Anne Loveland - *Pairings* (2012)

Olivia Stiffler - *Otherwise, we are safe* (2013)

Carole Stone - *Hurt, the Shadow-the Josephine Hopper poems* (2013)

Nathan Swartzendruber - *Opaque Projectionist* (2009)

Jean Syed - *Sonnets* (2009)

Madeline Tiger - *The Atheist's Prayer* (2010), *From the Viewing Stand* (2011)

James Tolan - *Red Walls* (2011)

Brian Volck - *Flesh Becomes Word* (2013)

Henry Weinfield - *The Tears of the Muses* (2005), *Without Mythologies* (2008), *A Wandering Aramaean* (2012)

Donald Wellman - *A North Atlantic Wall* (2010), *The Cranberry Island Series* (2012)

Sarah White - *The Unknowing Muse* (2014)

Anne Whitehouse - *The Refrain* (2012)

Martin Willetts Jr. - *Secrets No One Must Talk About* (2011)

Tyrone Williams - *Futures, Elections* (2004), *Adventures of Pi* (2011)

Kip Zegers - *The Poet of Schools* (2013)

www.dosmadres.com